THE OZONE LAYER

A TRUE BOOK

by

Rhonda Lucas Donald

Children's Press®
A Division of Scholastic Inc.

New York Toronto London Auckland Sydney
Mexico City New Delhi Hong Kong
Danbury, Connecticut

These people are protecting them-selves from the sun's harmful rays.

Reading Consultant
Linda Cornwell
*Coordinator of School Quality
and Professional Improvement
Indiana State
Teachers Association*

Content Consultant
Jan Jenner
*Rendalia Biologist
Talladega, AL*

*Author's Dedication:
For Ryan*

Library of Congress Cataloging-in-Publication Data

Donald, Rhonda Lucas, 1962–
    The ozone layer / by Rhonda Lucas Donald.
        p. cm. — (A true book)
    Includes bibliographical references and index.
    Summary: Explains how the ozone layer protects Earth from harmful
solar radiation and how ground-level ozone is a type of pollution.
    ISBN 0-516-22195-7 (lib.bdg.)   0-516-27355-8 (pbk.)
    1. Ozone Layer—Juvenile literature. 2. Ozone layer depletion—
Juvenile literature. [1. Ozone Layer. 2. Ozone layer depletion.] I. Title.
II. Series.
QC881.2. 09 D66 2001
551.51'42—dc21
                                                  00-038412

Contents

30 m

PROTECTIVE OZONE LAYER

STRATOSPHERE

TROPOSPHERE

10 m

SMOG

EARTH

The ozone layer protects Earth from the sun's harmful rays.

Ozone Is Good and Bad

More than 10 miles (16 kilometers) above the surface of Earth is a part of the atmosphere called the ozone layer. You cannot see the ozone layer because it is made of invisible gas. Earth's atmosphere is made up of many gases. One of them is oxygen, which people and animals need to breathe. Ozone is a type of oxygen that forms high in the atmosphere, but it is not a kind of oxygen that you can breathe.

The ozone layer does an important job. It absorbs many of the sun's harmful rays, keeping them from reaching the surface of Earth. You could say the ozone layer is like sunscreen for our planet! If you have

The ozone layer protects Earth from the sun's harmful rays like an umbrella protects you at the beach.

ever been sunburned, you know what happens when you stay out in the sun too long. Your skin burns because of the sun's harmful rays. Without the protecting ozone layer, you would sunburn more easily. More people would get diseases such as skin cancer. Some plants and animals might not be able to live any longer. The ozone layer helps protect the health of all living things.

The ozone layer helps these plants grow healthy and tall.

Not all ozone is created high in Earth's atmosphere, and not all ozone is beneficial. Some forms near the ground when pollution from cars and factories mixes with oxygen and sunlight. This low-down ozone is a type of air pollution. If you have seen smog—that sooty air that forms over cities—you have seen bad low-down ozone. Bad ozone can harm plants and animals. It even

Pollution from factories (left) makes bad ozone. Car exhaust is another cause of smog.

Bad ozone can be harmful to living things. Rubber tires (right) wear out faster because of bad ozone.

causes rubber to wear out faster. On hot summer days, some cities have to warn people to stay indoors because

TV smog warning.

there is so much smog. People
who have trouble breathing
because of lung disease are
most harmed by bad ozone.

Seeing the Invisible

How can you see the ozone layer if it is invisible? With a little help from a satellite that circles the Earth! Instruments on a satellite can measure the amount of ozone in the atmosphere. That helps scientists make a picture of what the ozone layer might look like. With the help of an ozone-measuring device called TOMS, scientists found a hole in the ozone layer over Antarctica—a hole that has grown larger and larger over the past 20 years.

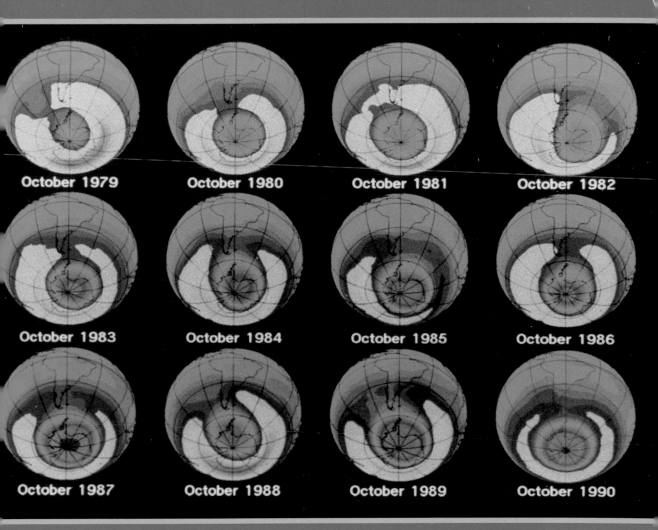

October 1979 October 1980 October 1981 October 1982

October 1983 October 1984 October 1985 October 1986

October 1987 October 1988 October 1989 October 1990

These TOMS (Total Ozone Mapping Spectrometer) images show the growing ozone hole over Antarctica.

Threats to the Ozone Layer

Ozone forms naturally in the atmosphere miles above Earth. After a time, ozone disappears, but more is created all the time. If man-made chemicals had never been produced, there would always be enough ozone to protect the Earth. Sadly, chemicals called

Spray cans used to contain CFCs, now they don't.

CFCs (chlorofluorocarbons) were developed, and they are ozone busters. CFCs were used in spray cans. In the past, manufacturers of foam packaging such as polystyrene foam used CFCs to make the foam. Factories have used CFCs to clean things like computer parts. Other ozone-busting chemicals are those that help make refrigerators and air conditioners cold, and halons, which you can find in some fire extinguishers and pesticides.

Ozone-busting chemicals rise up into the atmosphere. When they reach the ozone

Polystyrene foam used to be made using CFCs.

layer, the sun's energy breaks them up into molecules that eat up ozone. One ozone-busting molecule can gobble

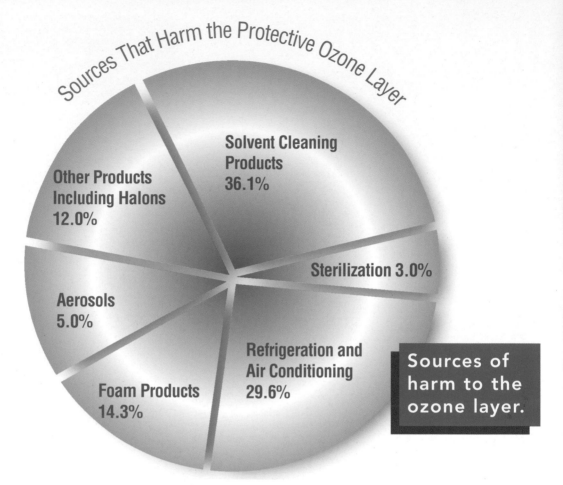

Solvent Cleaning Products 36.1%

Other Products Including Halons 12.0%

Sterilization 3.0%

Aerosols 5.0%

Refrigeration and Air Conditioning 29.6%

Foam Products 14.3%

Sources of harm to the ozone layer.

up 100,000 ozone molecules. Nature cannot replace the ozone fast enough to keep up with the ozone-busting molecules. The ozone layer is there-

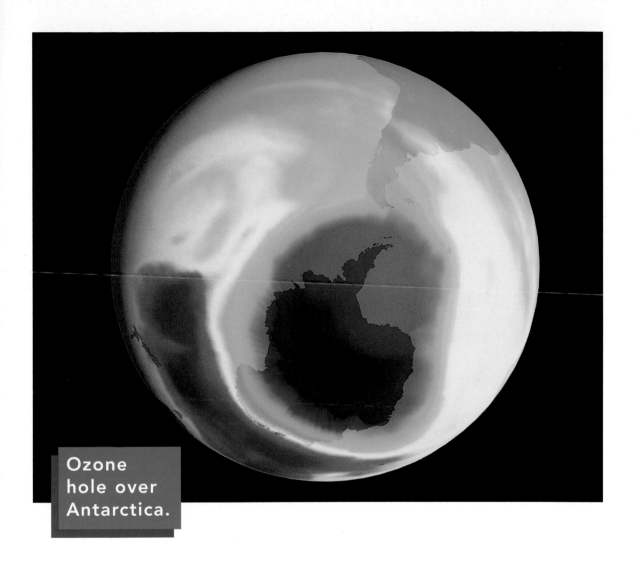

fore getting thinner. In the
atmosphere over Antarctica—
the continent at Earth's south

pole—there is already a huge ozone hole.

The ozone hole is not really empty. Rather, it is an area where the ozone layer is very thin. It may be thin, but it is big. It stretches nearly 10 million square miles (nearly 27.3 million square kilometers). That is as big as the North American continent! Another ozone hole has formed over the Arctic at Earth's north pole.

Colder air at the poles creates
molecules that harm the ozone layer.

An Arctic ozone hole could cause health and environmental problems for all the people of Europe. Ozone holes are forming at the ends of the Earth because the super cold temperatures and blasting winds at the poles speed up the creation of ozone-busting molecules.

What Happens Without the Ozone Layer?

In places where the ozone layer is thin, more of the sun's harmful rays can poke through and reach Earth. As a result, more people get skin cancer. In addition, the rays can slowly make people's eyesight less sharp and may prevent people

Be sure to wear sunscreen if you'll be in the sun for a long time.

from fighting off diseases. Because of the thinning ozone layer, scientists have warned people to use sunscreen and to wear protective clothing when outside. Long sleeves, hats,

and sunglasses can help protect you against harmful rays.

Many plants also suffer when
the ozone layer is not as
healthy as it should be. Some
crops, such as soybeans, cannot grow well when too many

Soybeans can be harmed by the sun without the ozone layer to protect them.

Fish like this whale shark feed on plankton (opposite).

of the sun's harmful rays reach them. The same is true for tiny ocean plants and animals called plankton.

Plankton feeds millions of sea creatures. Without plankton, many ocean animals would not have enough to eat.

The loss of the ozone layer can also lead to more bad ozone on Earth. Certain rays from the sun make smog worse. Without the good ozone layer above our planet, there could be more bad ozone down below. Protecting the ozone layer is important to all life on Earth.

Smog Days

Do you ever have snow days in which you get out of school? Some cities have "smog days," but schools usually stay open. On smog days, the air is so dirty that people should stay indoors and not drive their cars. Los Angeles, California, used to be the smog capital of the country. But in 1999, Houston, Texas, won the dishonor with the most smog days. The smog is even worse in Tehran, Iran. There the smog sometimes gets so bad that people wear masks to help them breathe.

Smog in Los Angeles.

Protecting the Ozone Layer

In 1989 leaders in more than 150 countries knew that they had to work together to stop ozone destruction. These leaders came up with ways to keep ozone-harming chemicals from getting into the atmosphere. One important way was to stop using CFCs. The United States

Spray cans no longer contain CFCs in the United States.

banned CFCs in spray cans long before, in 1978, but other countries still used them. Finally, many countries agreed to stop using CFCs altogether by 1995. Other countries have agreed to stop making CFCs in the future.

Healing the ozone layer will take some time. It takes several years for ozone busters to move through the atmosphere and reach the ozone layer. CFCs used five years ago may only now be damaging the ozone layer. Several years after no more harmful chemicals reach the ozone layer, it will begin to heal itself. If countries do away with CFCs and halons and take other steps to protect the ozone layer, it should begin to heal itself by the middle of this century.

You can help heal the ozone layer, too. First, talk to your parents and other adults about how important the ozone layer is. Then find out how to make sure no ozone-busting chemicals will reach the atmosphere. How?

• Check home and car air conditioners and refrigerators for chemical leaks. If there are leaks, have them fixed right away.

Have broken refrigerators or air conditioners fixed immediately.

Make sure that CFCs are safely collected and recycled.

• Be sure those who repair air conditioners and refrigerators do not let any harmful chemicals leak out. Technicians can safely collect and recycle CFCs without harming the ozone layer.

• When old air conditioners or refrigerators go bad, get rid of them properly. Your trash collector can tell you how.

Old refrigerators should be disposed of properly.

FRIDGES ONLY

A fire extinguisher with halons.

• Go on a halon hunt.
Organize your class at school
or your neighborhood friends
to search for fire extinguishers

that contain halons (look for "Halon" or "Halon 1211" on the label). Contact the extinguishers' manufacturers about turning in or exchanging them.

There is also a lot you can do to stop low-down ozone. Instead of riding in a car, walk, ride your bicycle, or take a bus or train to reduce ozone-causing pollution. Also ask adults to keep cars tuned up and to make

Ride your bike
instead of in a car.

Make sure cars and trucks have enough air in their tires.

sure there is enough air in the tires.

If everyone pitches in to protect the ozone layer, it will get healthy again. Then it will always be around to do its job as sunscreen for the planet!

To Find Out More

To learn more about the ozone layer, check out these resources:

 **Books**

Edmonds, Alex. **The Ozone Hole.** Cooper Beech Books, 1997.

Hare, Tony. **The Ozone Layer.** Gloucester Press, 1990.

Johnson, Rebecca. **Investigating the Ozone Hole.** Lerner Publishing, 1993.

Morgan, Sally. **The Ozone Hole.** Franklin Watts, 1999.

Pringle, Laurence. **Vanishing Ozone: Protecting Earth from Ultraviolet Radiation.** William Morrow, 1995.

Organizations and Online Sites

Environmental Protection Agency (EPA)
Public Information Center
401 M St., SW (TM-211B)
Washington, DC 20460
www.epa.gov/ozone

EPA has lots of information about good and bad ozone and a comic book, "On the Trail of the Missing Ozone," you can download.

Friends of the Earth (FOE)
1025 Vermont Ave., NW
Washington, DC 20005
*www.foe.org/ptp/
atmosphere*

"Healing the Atmosphere" is a section of FOE's web site with information about ozone-harming chemicals and ways you can help.

National Aeronautics and Space Administration (NASA)
Goddard Space Flight Center
8800 Greenbelt Rd.
Greenbelt, MD 20771
*http://jwocky.gsfc.nasa.
gov/multi/multi.html*

This NASA site has lots of video clips, pictures, and audio files about the ozone layer, the ozone hole, and a device called TOMS that helps scientists measure ozone. Another NASA site lets you see a map of the ozone layer over any location. It is at
*http://jwocky.gsfc.nasa.gov
/ozone01.html*

The Ozone Hole Tour
www.atm.ch.cam.ac.uk/tour

This web site features pictures and information about the ozone hole, how it is monitored, and ongoing research about the ozone layer.

Important Words

atmosphere the layer of air that surrounds Earth

cancer a disease in which harmful growths spread in the body

CFC a type of chemical that harms the ozone layer

halon a chemical found in some fire extinguishers and pesticides that harms the ozone layer

molecule a tiny bit of a chemical

ozone a layer of invisible gas in the atmosphere made of a type of oxygen that keeps some of the sun's harmful rays from reaching the Earth. Ozone at ground level is a type of pollution commonly called smog.

smog ozone at ground level that is a type of pollution

Index

Meet the Author

Rhonda Lucas Donald has written for children and teachers for fifteen years. Her work has appeared in magazines such as *Ranger Rick* and *Your Big Backyard*. She specializes in writing about science and natural history and creating projects that make these subjects fun. Rhonda received the EdPress award for best newsletter of 1997 for *EarthSavers*, an environmental newspaper and activity guide. She has also written several other environmental True Books for Children's Press. She lives in North Carolina with her husband, Bruce, cats Sophie and Tory, and Maggie the dog.

Photographs ©: AP/Wide World Photos: 11 bottom, 19; Corbis-Bettmann/Peter Johnson: 23; ImageBank/Simon Wilkinson: 26; Nance S. Trueworthy: 7, 12 right, 33, 39, 42; Peter Arnold Inc.: 28 (Kelvin Aitken), 9 (David Cavagnaro), 37 (Argus Fotoarchiv), 2 (Jodi Jacobson); Photo Researchers, NY: 12 left (Scott Camazine), 11 top (Tom Hollyman), 29 (George G. Lower), 8 (Susan McCartney), 1, 21 (NASA/SPL), cover (NOAA/SPL), 38 (SPL), 31 (David Weintraub); PhotoEdit: 36 (Myrleen Ferguson), 13 (David Young Wolfe); Photri Inc.: 41 (Fotopic), 15; U.S. EPA: 4, 20; Visuals Unlimited: 27 (Mark E. Gibson), 17 (Terry Gleason); author photo: Gerry Bishop.